THE FROZEN RIVER MYSTERY

A Tale of Betrayal and Redemption

Inspired by Ariel Lawhon

Joel O. Jorgenson

Copyright Page

Copyright © 2024 Joel O. Jorgenson

All rights reserved. No part of this publication may be reproduced, distributed, or transmitted in any form or by any means, including photocopying, recording, or other electronic or mechanical methods, without the prior written permission of the copyright holder, except in the case of brief quotations embodied in critical reviews and certain other noncommercial uses permitted by copyright law.

Preface

5 FAQs About *The* Frozen River

What is the main plot of The Frozen River?

- o The Frozen River is a historical fiction novel set in 18th-century Maine. It follows the story of Martha Ballard, a midwife, as she investigates the mysterious death of a prominent figure found frozen in the Kennebec River. The novel delves into themes of corruption, power, and the pursuit of truth.

Is The Frozen River based on a true story?

- o *While the novel is fictional, it is inspired by the real-life figure of Martha Ballard, a renowned midwife whose diary provides valuable historical insights. The story blends historical accuracy with a gripping fictional narrative.

What makes The Frozen River a compelling read?

- o *The novel offers a captivating blend of historical fiction and mystery. Its strong character development, vivid setting, and suspenseful plot make it a compelling read for fans of historical fiction and mystery alike. The exploration of themes such as the power of knowledge, the impact of secrets, and the role of women in 18th-century society adds depth and complexity to the story.

What is the significance of the frozen river in the novel?

- *The frozen river serves as both a physical and symbolic element in the story. It represents the harshness of the winter landscape and the frozen secrets of the past. It also symbolizes the frozen truth that lies beneath the surface of the town's seemingly peaceful existence.

What is the overall message of The Frozen River?

- *The novel conveys a powerful message about the importance of truth, justice, and the human spirit. It emphasizes the courage and resilience of individuals who dare to challenge the status quo and expose the darkness. Ultimately, The Frozen River is a story about the enduring power of hope and the triumph of good over evil.

TABLE OF CONTENT

THE DISCOVERY 7
The frozen Kennebec River 7
The discovery of the frozen body 10
Martha Ballard's initial involvement 11

A MYSTERIOUS MAN 13
The identity of the deceased 13
Rumors and speculations in the community 15
Martha's growing curiosity 16

A DARK SECRET 19
The deceased's past and connections 19
A hidden history of the town 20
The emergence of a dangerous secret 21

A DANGEROUS PATH 23
Martha's deepening investigation 23
The risks and consequences of her actions 24
The tension between personal safety and the pursuit of truth 26

A FRACTURED COMMUNITY 29
The impact of the mystery on the town 29

    Division and suspicion among the townspeople 30

    The erosion of trust and unity 31

A CHILLING REVELATION **33**

    The uncovering of a shocking truth 33

    The consequences of the revelation 35

    The resolution of the mystery 36

PERSONAL NOTES **38**

A Frozen River

THE DISCOVERY

The frozen Kennebec River

The Frozen River by Ariel Lawhon is a gripping historical mystery set in the harsh winter of 1789 in Hallowell, Maine. The novel is inspired by the real-life midwife Martha Ballard, whose diary provides a fascinating glimpse into the lives of ordinary people during this period.

A Mysterious Death

The story unfolds when a man is found frozen in the icy Kennebec River. Martha Ballard, a respected midwife and healer, is called upon to examine the body. As she delves deeper into the circumstances surrounding the death, she becomes entangled in a web of secrets, lies, and accusations.

A Community in Turmoil

The discovery of the frozen body sends shockwaves through the small town of Hallowell. Tensions rise as suspicions grow, and the community becomes divided. The local authorities, eager to maintain order, are quick to dismiss the incident as an unfortunate accident. However, Martha, with her keen observation and unwavering determination, believes that there is more to the story.

A Woman's Perspective

One of the strengths of "The Frozen River" is its portrayal of women in 18th-century America. Martha Ballard is a complex and compelling character who defies societal expectations. She is a skilled midwife, a wise counselor, and a fearless truth-seeker. Through her eyes, we see the challenges and limitations faced by women during this era.

The Power of the Written Word

Martha's diary serves as a crucial piece of evidence in the investigation. Her meticulous records of births, deaths, and community events provide valuable insights into the lives of the townspeople. The diary also highlights the importance of literacy and the power of the written word in shaping history.

Historical Accuracy

Lawhon's meticulous research brings 18th-century Maine to life. The novel accurately depicts the harsh winter conditions, the challenges of daily life, and the social and political climate of the time. The inclusion of historical details, such as the use of herbal remedies and traditional healing practices, adds depth and authenticity to the story.

Themes of Justice and Redemption

"The Frozen River" explores themes of justice, redemption, and the enduring power of human spirit. Martha's unwavering pursuit of truth challenges the status quo and inspires others to stand up for what is right. The novel also delves into the complexities of human nature, highlighting the capacity for both good and evil.

A Gripping Read

Lawhon's masterful storytelling draws readers into the heart of 18th-century Maine. The suspenseful plot, combined with the vivid historical setting, makes "The Frozen River" a captivating read. Whether you are a fan of historical fiction or simply enjoy a good mystery, this book is sure to captivate you.

The discovery of the frozen body

The frozen Kennebec River, a silent, icy expanse, held a chilling secret. As the bitter winter of 1789 gripped Hallowell, Maine, a gruesome discovery shattered the town's tranquility. A frozen body, encased in ice, emerged from the river's depths, its identity a mystery, its cause of death a haunting question mark.

Martha Ballard, a respected midwife and healer, was summoned to examine the remains. With a keen eye and a steady hand, she meticulously inspected the body, her mind racing as she pieced together the fragments of a chilling puzzle. The man, later identified as Joshua Burgess, a prominent figure in the community, bore the unmistakable marks of violence.

As Martha delved deeper into the circumstances surrounding Burgess's death, she found herself drawn into a web of secrets, lies, and accusations. The town, once united, now fractured into factions, each with their own theories and suspicions. The local authorities, eager to maintain order, were quick to dismiss the incident as an unfortunate accident. However, Martha, with her unwavering determination and keen observation, believed that there was more to the story.

The discovery of the frozen body ignited a fire within Martha, a burning desire to uncover the truth. She knew that the answers lay hidden beneath the surface, buried beneath layers of deceit and corruption. With each passing day, the stakes grew higher, and the danger more imminent. But Martha was undeterred. She was a woman of courage, a woman of conviction, and she would not rest until justice was served.

Martha Ballard's initial involvement

Martha Ballard, a respected midwife and healer in Hallowell, Maine, was initially drawn into the mystery surrounding the frozen body due to her unique position in the community. As a woman who regularly crossed the frozen Kennebec River to tend to her patients, she was well-acquainted with its treacherous nature. Moreover, her reputation as a skilled observer and meticulous record-keeper made her a valuable asset in any investigation.

When news of the frozen body reached her, Martha was immediately intrigued. The unusual circumstances of the death piqued her curiosity, and she volunteered to examine the remains. With a keen eye and a steady hand, she meticulously inspected the body, noting every detail, no matter how small. Her sharp mind quickly began to piece together the fragments of a chilling puzzle.

As she delved deeper into the investigation, Martha's involvement grew. She interviewed witnesses, examined evidence, and consulted with local authorities. Her insights and observations proved invaluable, as she brought a fresh perspective to the case. However, her growing involvement also put her in danger, as she began to uncover secrets that some people would rather keep hidden.

A MYSTERIOUS MAN

The identity of the deceased

The frozen body pulled from the icy depths of the Kennebec River was that of Joshua Burgess, a prominent figure in the small town of Hallowell, Maine. Burgess was known for his wealth, his influence, and his rather unsavory reputation.

His death sent shockwaves through the community, and the circumstances surrounding it were shrouded in mystery. The official cause of death was declared to be accidental drowning, but many in the town harbored doubts. Martha Ballard, a keen observer and skilled midwife, was one of those who suspected foul play.

Burgess had been implicated in a recent scandal involving the rape of Rebecca Foster, the wife of the local reverend. The accusation had tarnished his reputation and brought shame upon his family. The townspeople were divided, some believing in Burgess's innocence, others convinced of his guilt. The discovery of his frozen body only added fuel to the fire of speculation.

As Martha delved deeper into the investigation, she uncovered a web of secrets and lies that connected Burgess to a darker side of Hallowell. She learned about his involvement in illicit activities, his questionable business dealings, and his penchant for exploiting the vulnerable. It became clear that Burgess was not the upstanding citizen he portrayed himself to be.

The identity of the deceased, Joshua Burgess, proved to be a key piece in the puzzle of the town's dark secrets. His death, far from being a simple accident, was a catalyst for uncovering a web of corruption and injustice. Martha's relentless pursuit of the truth led her to confront the powerful and challenge the status quo. As she peeled back the layers of deceit, she risked her own life to expose the truth and bring justice to those who had been wronged.

Rumors and speculations in the community

The discovery of Joshua Burgess's frozen body ignited a firestorm of rumors and speculations throughout Hallowell, Maine. The townspeople, eager for answers, began to weave tales that painted a picture of a man far different from the one they had known.

Some whispered that Burgess had been involved in a secret society, a clandestine group that met in the dead of night to plot and scheme. Others claimed he had made a powerful enemy, someone who sought revenge for a past wrong. Still others suggested that his death was a sacrifice to a dark force, a chilling ritual carried out under the cover of darkness.

As the rumors spread, fear and paranoia gripped the community. People looked at each other with suspicion, wondering who among them might be harboring dark secrets. The once peaceful town became a place of fear and mistrust, where shadows seemed to lurk around every corner.

Martha Ballard, with her keen eye and sharp mind, was not immune to the rumors. She knew that the truth was often stranger than fiction, and that the darkest secrets were often hidden in plain sight. As she delved deeper into the investigation, she began to realize that the answer to the mystery of Burgess's death might be more shocking than anyone could have imagined.

Martha's growing curiosity

Martha Ballard, a seasoned midwife and healer, was a woman of keen observation and an insatiable curiosity. As she delved deeper into the mysterious death of Joshua Burgess, her curiosity grew with each passing day. The more she learned about the man, the more questions arose.

She was intrigued by the conflicting accounts of his character. Some described him as a generous benefactor, while others painted him as a ruthless opportunist. The contradictions piqued her interest, prompting her to seek out the truth, no matter where it led.

Martha's curiosity was further fueled by the strange circumstances surrounding Burgess's death. The official explanation of accidental drowning seemed too simplistic, too convenient. The more she examined the evidence, the more she doubted the veracity of the authorities' conclusion.

Her growing curiosity led her to explore the darker corners of Hallowell, venturing into places she had never been before. She spoke with people from all walks of life, from the town's elite to its most marginalized citizens. Each conversation provided a new piece of the puzzle, a new clue to unravel.

As she pieced together the fragments of the truth, Martha realized that she was treading on dangerous ground. The more she learned, the more she became a target for those who sought to silence her. Yet, her determination remained unwavering. She was determined to uncover the truth, no matter the cost.

A DARK SECRET

The deceased's past and connections

As Martha delved deeper into the life of Joshua Burgess, she began to uncover a web of secrets and connections that extended far beyond the confines of Hallowell. His past was shrouded in mystery, with rumors of questionable dealings and dubious alliances.

It was rumored that Burgess had ties to a secret society, a clandestine group that operated in the shadows, pulling the strings of power. This shadowy organization was said to be involved in a variety of illicit activities, from smuggling to extortion. Burgess's involvement with this group could have made him a target for enemies both within and outside the organization.

Furthermore, Burgess had a history of exploiting the vulnerable, particularly women. He had been accused of taking advantage of young girls, promising them wealth and security in exchange for their silence. His predatory behavior had earned him the ire of many, and it was possible that one of his victims, or someone close to them, had sought revenge.

As Martha pieced together the fragments of Burgess's past, she realized that his death was not an isolated incident. It was a symptom of a deeper malaise, a corruption that had taken root in the heart of Hallowell. She knew that to uncover the truth, she would have to confront the darkness that lurked beneath the town's seemingly peaceful facade.

A hidden history of the town

As Martha delved deeper into the history of Hallowell, she uncovered a hidden past, a dark secret that had been buried for generations. The town, once a beacon of Puritan virtue, had a darker side, a side that few people knew about.

Beneath the veneer of respectability, a web of corruption and deceit had taken root. Powerful families, driven by greed and ambition, had manipulated the town's affairs for their own benefit. They had used their influence to silence dissent, to suppress the truth, and to maintain their grip on power.

Martha discovered that the town's founders had arrived with a hidden agenda, a desire to establish a new world order, a world free from the constraints of traditional morality. They had brought with them a secret doctrine, a belief system that justified their actions, no matter how heinous.

As she uncovered the town's hidden history, Martha realized that she was not just investigating a murder. She was uncovering a conspiracy, a plot to control the minds and bodies of the townspeople. The more she learned, the more she realized that her life was in danger.

The emergence of a dangerous secret

As Martha delved deeper into the hidden history of Hallowell, she stumbled upon a dangerous secret, a secret that could unravel the very fabric of the town. The more she uncovered, the more she realized that her life was in danger.

She discovered that the town's founders had brought with them a dark secret, a secret that threatened to destroy the lives of innocent people. This secret, a sinister plot to control the minds and bodies of the townspeople, had been passed down through generations, a silent curse that haunted the town.

Martha's investigation led her to a hidden room in the town's old library, a room that had been sealed for centuries. Inside, she found a collection of ancient texts, filled with cryptic symbols and forbidden knowledge. These texts revealed the true nature of the secret society, a group of powerful individuals who sought to dominate the world.

As she delved deeper into the texts, Martha realized that she was not just uncovering a historical mystery. She was uncovering a conspiracy, a plot that could have far-reaching consequences. The more she learned, the more she became a target for those who sought to silence her. She knew that her life was in danger, but she was determined to uncover the truth, no matter the cost.

A Thawed Truth

A DANGEROUS PATH

Martha's deepening investigation

Martha Ballard, undeterred by the growing danger, pressed on with her investigation. Each new clue, each new lead, took her deeper into the heart of darkness. She knew that the truth was out there, hidden beneath layers of deception and lies.

She spent countless hours poring over old documents, interviewing witnesses, and following shadowy figures. Her relentless pursuit of the truth led her to the fringes of society, where she encountered individuals who lived outside the law. These people, though often feared and reviled, held the key to unlocking the mystery of Joshua Burgess's death.

Martha's investigation took her to the darkest corners of Hallowell, where she witnessed the town's hidden underbelly. She saw the desperation, the despair, and the violence that lurked beneath the surface. She realized that the town's idyllic facade was merely a mask, a carefully constructed illusion that hid a sinister reality.

As she delved deeper into the investigation, Martha began to understand the true nature of the conspiracy. She realized that the death of Joshua Burgess was just one piece of a much larger puzzle. The town's leaders, the men who held the reins of power, were involved in a sinister plot to control the minds and bodies of the townspeople.

The more she learned, the more dangerous her situation became. She was being watched, followed, and threatened. But Martha was not afraid. She knew that the truth was worth fighting for, even if it meant risking her life.

The risks and consequences of her actions

Martha Ballard's relentless pursuit of the truth put her life in grave danger. As she delved deeper into the shadowy world of Hallowell's secrets, she became a target for those who sought to silence her. The powerful and influential individuals who controlled the town's destiny would stop at nothing to protect their interests.

Every step she took brought her closer to the edge, closer to the precipice. She faced the constant threat of violence, intimidation, and even death. Her reputation was tarnished, her family was threatened, and her livelihood was put at risk. Yet, she pressed on, driven by a sense of justice and a commitment to truth.

The consequences of her actions were far-reaching. Her investigation not only endangered her own life but also the lives of those closest to her. Her family, her friends, and her community were caught in the crossfire, forced to bear the brunt of the backlash from her relentless pursuit of the truth.

The townspeople, once united, were now divided. Some saw her as a hero, a champion of justice, while others saw her as a threat, a disruptor of the peace. The lines between friend and foe blurred, and trust was eroded. The once peaceful town of Hallowell was transformed into a battleground, where the forces of good and evil clashed.

The tension between personal safety and the pursuit of truth

Martha Ballard found herself torn between two conflicting desires: her personal safety and her unwavering pursuit of the truth. As she delved deeper into the dark secrets of Hallowell, the tension between these two forces intensified.

On one hand, she yearned for a peaceful life, a life free from danger and fear. She longed to tend to her patients, to raise her family, and to enjoy the simple pleasures of life. However, her conscience would not allow her to ignore the injustice and corruption that plagued her community.

On the other hand, she was driven by a powerful sense of duty. She believed that it was her responsibility to expose the truth, no matter the cost. She knew that by remaining silent, she would be complicit in the oppression of others.

The tension between these two forces created a constant internal struggle. She often questioned her decision to continue the investigation, wondering if the risks outweighed the rewards. Yet, each time she considered abandoning her pursuit, she was reminded of the victims, the innocent people who had suffered at the hands of the powerful.

Ultimately, Martha's unwavering commitment to justice prevailed. She chose to risk her life to expose the truth, to bring light to the darkness. She knew that the path ahead would be fraught with danger, but she was determined to see it through to the end.

A FRACTURED COMMUNITY

The impact of the mystery on the town

The discovery of Joshua Burgess's frozen body sent shockwaves through the quiet town of Hallowell, Maine. The once peaceful community was thrown into turmoil, as fear and suspicion gripped the hearts of its inhabitants. The mystery surrounding Burgess's death cast a long shadow over the town, disrupting the delicate balance of power and privilege.

As the investigation unfolded, the townspeople found themselves caught in a web of intrigue and danger. The lines between friend and foe blurred, and trust was eroded. Neighbors turned against neighbors, and old friendships were strained. The once tight-knit community became fractured, divided by fear and suspicion.

The mystery also had a profound impact on the town's economy. The influx of outsiders, including investigators and journalists, disrupted the normal course of business. The fear and uncertainty that permeated the town discouraged visitors and deterred potential investors.

Moreover, the town's reputation was tarnished. The news of the mysterious death spread far and wide, painting a picture of a town plagued by violence and corruption. This negative publicity had a detrimental effect on the town's image, making it difficult to attract new residents and businesses.

Division and suspicion among the townspeople

The discovery of Joshua Burgess's frozen body ignited a firestorm of rumors and accusations, tearing the once-harmonious community of Hallowell apart. As the investigation unfolded, the townspeople found themselves divided into factions, each with their own theories and suspicions.

Some believed that Burgess's death was a tragic accident, a result of a misstep on a dark and icy night. Others, however, suspected foul play, whispering about dark secrets and hidden agendas. The townspeople began to eye each other with suspicion, questioning their motives and loyalties.

Old friendships were strained, and new alliances formed. Neighbors turned against neighbors, and families were torn apart. The once tight-knit community became a battleground of conflicting opinions and accusations. The air was thick with tension, and the fear of the unknown loomed large.

As Martha Ballard delved deeper into the mystery, she became a target for both admiration and scorn. Some saw her as a hero, a champion of truth and justice. Others, however, viewed her as a threat, a disruptor of the peace. The townspeople were divided, unable to agree on whether she was a savior or a villain.

The erosion of trust and unity

The discovery of Joshua Burgess's frozen body had a profound impact on the social fabric of Hallowell, Maine. The once tight-knit community, characterized by trust and unity, began to unravel as fear and suspicion took hold.

As the investigation unfolded, the townspeople found themselves questioning the motives of those around them. Old friendships were strained, and new alliances formed. The once-harmonious community became a battleground of conflicting opinions and accusations.

The erosion of trust was further exacerbated by the influx of outsiders. Investigators, journalists, and curious onlookers descended upon the town, disrupting the peace and privacy of its inhabitants. The townspeople, already on edge, became even more wary of strangers, fearing that they might be spies or informants.

The loss of unity had a devastating impact on the town's social and economic well-being. The once vibrant community spirit was replaced by a sense of isolation and distrust. The town's reputation was tarnished, and its future uncertain. As the townspeople struggled to come to terms with the tragedy, they realized that the healing process would be long and arduous.

A CHILLING REVELATION

The uncovering of a shocking truth

As Martha delved deeper into the mystery surrounding Joshua Burgess's death, she uncovered a shocking truth that would shake the foundations of Hallowell. The seemingly accidental drowning was, in fact, a carefully orchestrated murder, a sinister act carried out by a powerful group of individuals who sought to maintain their grip on power.

The key to unlocking this dark secret lay in the town's hidden history, a history that was shrouded in secrecy and deceit. Martha discovered that a secret society, a clandestine group of wealthy and influential individuals, had been manipulating the town's affairs for generations. This group, known as the "Silent Hand," had a vested interest in maintaining the status quo, and they would stop at nothing to protect their interests.

The Silent Hand had targeted Joshua Burgess because he had threatened to expose their corrupt practices. They had lured him to the frozen river, where they carried out their deadly plan. The carefully staged scene of an accidental drowning was meant to mislead the authorities and protect the culprits from suspicion.

As Martha pieced together the evidence, she realized that she was in grave danger. The Silent Hand would stop at nothing to silence her, to eliminate any threat to their power. She knew that her life was on the line, but she was determined to bring the truth to light, no matter the cost.

The consequences of the revelation

The revelation of the truth about Joshua Burgess's murder sent shockwaves through the town of Hallowell. The once peaceful community was thrown into chaos as the townspeople grappled with the reality of the dark secrets that had been hidden for so long.

The exposure of the Silent Hand's sinister activities led to a wave of arrests and prosecutions. Powerful individuals were brought to justice, and the corrupt system that had oppressed the town for generations was dismantled. However, the damage had already been done. The town's reputation was tarnished, and its social fabric was irreparably torn.

Martha Ballard, the woman who had brought the truth to light, became a symbol of hope and resilience. She was hailed as a hero, a champion of justice who had dared to challenge the powerful. However, her victory came at a great cost. She had faced threats, intimidation, and even attempts on her life. Her unwavering courage and determination had made her a target for the vengeful forces of darkness.

The aftermath of the revelation was a period of healing and rebuilding. The town of Hallowell, though scarred by the past, emerged stronger and more united. The people, inspired by Martha's courage, vowed to create a future free from corruption and injustice.

The resolution of the mystery

With relentless determination, Martha Ballard pieced together the final pieces of the puzzle. She uncovered the truth about the Silent Hand and their role in Joshua Burgess's murder. The evidence was irrefutable: the respected members of the community, those who held the reins of power, were the very ones who had orchestrated the crime.

The revelation sent shockwaves through the town. The townspeople, once blinded by the facade of respectability, were horrified by the depths of corruption that had taken root in their midst. The Silent Hand's carefully constructed image crumbled, exposing the dark reality beneath.

With the truth exposed, justice began to prevail. The guilty were brought to trial and punished for their crimes. The town, once divided and fearful, began to heal. The people, inspired by Martha's courage and resilience, united to rebuild their community and create a brighter future.

Martha's tireless efforts to uncover the truth had transformed her from a humble midwife to a symbol of hope and justice. Her legacy would forever be etched in the annals of Hallowell's history, a testament to the power of one person to challenge the darkness and bring light to the world.

PERSONAL NOTES

www.ingramcontent.com/pod-product-compliance
Lightning Source LLC
LaVergne TN
LVHW010935090225
803311LV00012B/1086